1	16ˣ	31	47ˣˣ	63	79	95	111	126	143	161	129	196
1ᴬ	16	31ᴬ	47ˣ	64	79ᴬ	95ᴬ	111ᴬ	127	144	162	179ᴬ	196ᴬ
2	17	32	47	64ᴬ	80	96	112	128	145	162ˣ	180ˣ	197
3	18	33	48	65	81	97	112ᴬ	129	146	162ᴬ	180	197ᴬ
4	19	33ᴬ	48ᴬ	66	82	97ᴬ	113	129ᴬ		162ᴮ	180ᴬ	198
5	20	34	48ᴮ	67	82ᴬ	98	113ᴬ	130	147	162ᶜ	181	198ᴬ
6	20ᴬ	35	49	68	83	99	113ᴮ	131	148	163	182	199
7	21	36	50	69	84	99ᴬ	114	132	149	166	183	199ᴬ
8	22	37	51ᴬ	70	85	99ᴮ	115	132ᴬ	150ˣˣ	167	184	200
9	23	38	51ᴮ	71	86	99ᶜ	116	133	160ˣ	171	185	201
10	24	39	51ᶜ	72	86ᴬ	99ᴰ	116	133ᴬ	160ˣ	171ᴬ	186	202
11	25	40	51ᴰ	73	87	101	118ᴬ	134	150	172	186ᴬ	202ᴬ
12	26	41	51ᴱ	74	87ᴬ	102	119	135	151	173	187	203
13	27	42	54	75	88	102ᴬ	119ᴬ	136	152	174	187ᴬ	204
14	28	43	56	76	90	103	120	137	153	174ᴬ	188	205
15	28ᴬ	44	57	77	90ᴮ	104	120ᴬ	138	154	175	189	206
15ᴬ	29	45	58	78	91	105	121	138ᴬ	155	175ᴬ	190	207
	30	46	59		91ᴬ	106	122	139	156	176	191	212
			60		92	107	122ᴬ	139ᴬ	156ᴬ	177	192ˣ	213
			61		92ᴮ	108	123	140	156ᴮ	90ᴬ	192	214
			62		93	109	123ᴬ	140ᴬ		178	192ᴬ	215
					93ᴬ	110	124	141			193	216
											193ᴬ	217
											194	
											195	

DESIGNS FOR CHURCH EMBROIDERY

DESIGNS

FOR

CHURCH EMBROIDERY

BY

A. R.

LETTERPRESS BY

ALETHEA WIEL

LONDON: CHAPMAN AND HALL, LIMITED.

1894.

LONDON:
PRINTED BY WILLIAM CLOWES AND SONS, LIMITED,
STAMFORD STREET AND CHARING CROSS.

𝕮o my 𝔣rieno

ALETHEA WIEL,

THE DESIGNS IN THIS VOLUME

ARE

𝕯edicateo

BY

A. R.

Introduction.

✤

In the following designs here offered to the public there is no claim to present more than a bare outline of ideas. A. R., the originator of all the designs, has spent some years over the work, and she disclaims for any pretence to finish or elaboration, maintaining that they are merely suggestions and hints for Church Embroidery, with the sole merit (surely no small one) that every design is original, though now and again some picture or flower has suggested an idea, whose embodiment she has afterwards carried out according to her own originality and fancy.

The thought of publishing these designs did not occur to A. R., who looked upon her collection as too incomplete for such a purpose, till she was persuaded to do so by the ever-increasing need for such outlines for workers of Church Embroidery, and by the advice of friends who she felt were better judges on such matters than herself. She consequently offers the work to the public, fully conscious of its shortcomings, and only hoping that her aim of adding, in however small a degree, to the worship of that King whose service should ever be encircled with the Beauty of holiness may not be in vain, and that her small volume may eventually fulfil its mission.

The colour card at the beginning of the book has been inserted by the kind permission of Messrs. Liberty & Co., of Regent Street, London; and A. R. cannot say enough in praise of their colours and Filo Floss silks sold by them. Many of the colours, she says, are perfect; and this verdict is made after comparing them with many original pictures of the old masters in Italy and elsewhere—the shades of red, green, blue, and browns being spoken of with special praise.

The "Church Times," speaking of the Church Congress in October, 1888, says: "There was some really very fine original embroidery designed and lent by A. R., of South Raynham, Norfolk; the coral grapes, which were worked in with the design, were very striking and effective. There was also an exquisite stole in etching work, St. John at one end and St. Thomas Aquinas at the other, also by same hand. The Sisters of St. Catherine, 32, Queen Square, Bloomsbury, had worked the last mentioned, also the stole for St. Michael and All Angels, for the Church of St. Michael, Folkestone, which gave great satisfaction. The designs were all roughly sketched by H. R., but the work of drawing them out correctly for the press has been carefully done by Mr. Oswald Fleuss. Full-sized drawings on paper, or any material for embroidering, should such be required. For particulars apply to H. R., 18, Warwick Square, London, S.W.

Index.

✤

Sizes of Chalice Veils, Stoles, &c.

✠

Stole, "Eucharistic" - - 3 yards in length, 3 inches in width.

„ Preaching - - - 2 yards 6 inches in length.

Chalice Veil - - - - 20 to 22 inches square.

Burse - - - - - 9 inches square.

✠

Correct patterns of Chasubles, Copes, and all Vestments can be supplied, cut out in calico, for 7/6 each, by writing, enclosing P. O., to A. R., 18, Warwick Square, London, S.W.

For Chalice Veils. It represents our Lord pointing to His heart to express what He has borne for those He loves, is surrounded by grapes and passion flowers, while in His right hand He holds the wafer and chalice, upon which the Holy Dove is pouring down the sanctifying rays of consecration.

This design would also lend itself well to a Burse if the flowers and fruit were worked all over it, or some other figure substituted in place of that of our Lord in the middle.

This design is for a Chalice Veil. In the centre stands the Agnus Dei, upheld by four angels, who have put down their musical instruments, and standing on them, have taken up instead the instruments of the Passion, upholding with their right hands the Agnus Dei. The four streams suggest the Psalmist's words: "There is a river, the streams whereof shall make glad the city of God." See too Ezekiel xlvii. Observe the beauty of this design when placed over the Chalice: the four angels stand around, guarding at each quarter the sacred element.

Is again intended for a Chalice Veil. A Chalice stands on seven small rocks, which represent the seven Sacraments: Baptism, St. Matt. xxviii. 19; Confirmation, Acts viii. 17; Eucharist, St. Matt. xxvi. 26; Penance, St. John xx. 23; Extreme Unction, St. James v. 14; Holy Orders, St. Luke xxii. 29; Matrimony, St. Matt. xix. 6.

Engraved on the Chalice is the Nativity, while rising, as it were, out of the Cup is a figure of our Lord representing the Blessed Sacrament. On each side of Him kneel two Angels with incense burners, and in each corner, under a spray of vine, fruit, and leaves, are placed St. Luke and St. John, with their attendant emblems.

Turning to the other side of the Veil, we find

the Crucifixion, from which two angels are turning away, trying with part of their wings to screen from their eyes the sight of the suffering of the Son of God. St. Matthew and St. Mark are placed, with their emblems, at each corner. The vine, which we noticed at the other side, is the emblem of our Lord ("I am the true vine"—John xv. 1), and of the Blessed Sacrament; and, perhaps, it is only when we realise how the vine is not allowed to come to maturity, or even be of use, till after it has undergone endless pruning, cutting, treading under foot, and perfecting through suffering that we grasp how fit an emblem it can be to our earth= born comprehensions of Him who has sanctified and ennobled suffering above all else here below.

The Chalice Veil, for which No. 4 is designed, is a most lovely arrangement of grapes, leaves, and flowers, to which is added a representation of the sacramental grace poured forth by the Holy Spirit on a beautiful trio of angels, who stand as symbols of all those who come in the wedding garment to the marriage supper of the Lamb.

The grapes should be worked in real coral, with the leaves outlined in green and gold. The flowers to be done in cream colour, and the branches heavily worked in gold.

No. 5.

The following drawing is for an Altar Frontal, wherein the seven doves represent the seven gifts of the Holy Ghost. In the central panel is the Good Shepherd, bearing the crook, and with the lamb in His arms; while the side panels contain the lily of purity and the palm of martyrdom. The super=frontal is simple, relieved only by the crown in the centre, and a cross with the nimbus on each side.

No. 6.

No. 6 forms the other half of the Stole, and is a beautiful representation of the "harmony, the heavenly harmony, and"

"Notes inspiring holy love,
Notes that wing their heavenly ways
To mend the choir above,"

and bid us raise our thoughts to the glorious company of apostles, prophets, martyrs, and all angels, who, 'mid music and incense, present an unceasing offering of prayer and praise to Him that sits on the Throne, and to the Lamb for ever and ever.

For a Stole specially adapted for St. Michael and All Saints, and other Saints' days. St. Michael stands weighing souls, while above the Blessed Virgin is seen with the Holy Babe in her arms, throwing her rosary into the scale, to outweigh the other scale, at which the Devil is pulling vigorously. St. Michael, certain of victory, stands triumphantly on the dragon, grasping in his right hand his lance and a banner, on which is represented the Holy Spirit as a dove.

These are designs for a Stole. In No. 8 we have all the emblems of the Blessed Virgin, with the back=ground formed of an apple tree, on which are suspended five shields, the uppermost bearing the sacred monogram for "Christ"; the next two representing "Yea, a sword shall pierce through thine own heart also," and the offering of two turtle doves; whilst below is represented the second Eve treading on the serpent to crush out the evil done by the first Eve ("thou shalt bruise his heel"), and the lily, the flower sacred to the blessed Virgin Mary, and emblematical of purity.

No. 9 forms the companion to No. 8, and consists of the vine supporting the five shields, on which are drawn all the instruments of our Lord's Passion.

No. 8.   No. 9.

This second half of a Stole, forming a companion to the expulsion of Adam and Eve from the Garden of Eden, represents the return of the Prodigal Son, and the welcome of his father to the child whom he had considered dead, and who is now restored from a death of sin and guilt to the new birth of righteousness.

The swine whom he has tended (and whose thriving condition is in marked contrast to the rags and leanness of their former keeper) are shown as under his feet, since he has now forsaken the paths of ungodliness, and is restored to the sonship which he had forfeited while in the service of sin.

In the middle distance stands the fatted calf, unconscious as yet of the part it will soon have to play in the festivities of mirth and gladness for the home=coming of one who was dead and is alive again, and who was lost and is found.

This design for a Stole shows our first parents being driven out of Paradise, and contains many and varied mystical symbols, together with plain representations of the sin that through Eve's transgression crept into the world. Adam, clothed in the skins of beasts, would seem to speak words of consolation to his wife, into whose soul the iron has entered, and who refuses to be comforted. As though to demonstrate, however, the first movement towards repentance, she has thrown away in disgust the apple out of which one bitten morsel brought such sorrow and suffering upon her and all her race.

The serpent hisses in derision at their feet, forgetful of the fact that his malignity is to be swallowed up in victory by the Lion of Judah, crouching only till the fulness of time; and regardless of the rays of the Sun of Righteousness, foreshadowed in the background as rising over the world, which shall be saved when the Church of Christ, represented · by the phœnix, shall have triumphed over sin and death.

Two halves of a Stole. The Christ of the Greek Church of Alexandria, introduced into Europe by the Empress Helena. He is crowned as king, vested with the seamless robe or alb, and chasuble over; the arms extended straight ("It was His will, not the nails, that kept Him there"). He represents the Prophet, Priest, and King. Each side are seven candlesticks, typical of the union of the Hebrew and the Christian Church. Above, are Angels, holding emblems of the Passion. Over the Divine Head, the Holy Ghost resting in the form of a dove, and surmounted by an angel blowing the golden horn.

On the other side, the Blessed Mother, with her lily each side of her, and the Angels holding various emblems of her—the doves of her Purification, the sword which pierced through her soul, the apples of Eve's fall. She holds in her hands the fish and a jug for watering her lilies.

No. 12.   No. 13.

No. 14 represents St. John the Evangelist, with the Holy Spirit as a dove descending on him, and reflecting too the beatific rays which emanate from the Blessed Sacrament held in the Evangelist's right hand, while his left is raised in blessing.

On his right are grouped his emblems: an eagle, an open book, and a sword, around which is twined a serpent. A cherub kneels at his feet, holding the ink=horn and pen, with which the Apostle of Love is to record his vision to the seven churches, and his message of love and charity to the world at large.

No. 14.

The other half of the design for a Stole, and which forms a pendant to St. John the Evangelist, is St. Thomas Aquinas in the act of offering up his book to our Lord on the cross.

An old French manuscript thus relates the legend here represented: "As the clock struck the hour of twelve from the cloister bell, St. Thomas stood with his finished work in front of the altar, and offering it up with a prayer of dedication to the Blessed Trinity, according to Tocco and others, Domenico Casate beheld him while in fervent prayer raised from the ground, and heard a voice from the crucifix directed to him in these words: 'Thou hast written well of Me, Thomas; what recompense dost thou desire?' He answered, 'No other than Thyself, O Lord.'"

S · THOMAS · AQUINAS ·

This design, composed chiefly of the emblems belonging to the Holy Ghost, of the lily of purity, the star of wisdom and understanding, and the crown of counsel and might, is suitable for Bookmarkers, Stoles, &c.; and can also be adapted for Altar Frontals, or for Vestments.

This design, adapted from one found on a tomb in the Catacombs in Rome, can be used for the ends of Stoles, Burses, Chalice Veils, &c., &c.

The three circles denote the Trinity, "Three in One"; the triangle itself representing the nimbus of God the Father, and found in late Italian and Greek art; the lamb representing God the Son; and the dove, God the Holy Ghost.

These circles recall to our mind the words of Dante, when, speaking of the Blessed Trinity, he says how the vision appeared to him:

> "In that abyss
> Of radiance, clear and lofty, seem'd, methought,
> Three orbs of triple hue, clift in one bound:
> And, from another, one reflected seem'd,
> As rainbow is from rainbow: and the third
> Seem'd fire, breathed equally from both."

PARADISE, *Canto xxxiii.*, *v.* 116, *etc.*, *Cary's Tr.*

This design for a Burse would also make a lovely Chalice Veil. The four angels with trumpets in one hand and holding a banner with the emblems of the four Evangelists; in the centre, the vine, and chalice, and host.

No. 19.

This stiff design of flowers and leaves is one
easy of execution, and adaptable to any purpose.
It will serve equally reduced or enlarged, according
to fancy.

This "Valley" design is suitable to work all over, for instance, an Altar Frontal, a Cope, or Chasuble. Called "the valley," because the idea came from studying "lilies of the valley." The stalks to be done in gold and silk over string, the bells to be in gold, but, as with several of the others, it must be left very much to the ideas of the worker. There are very many ways of working it.

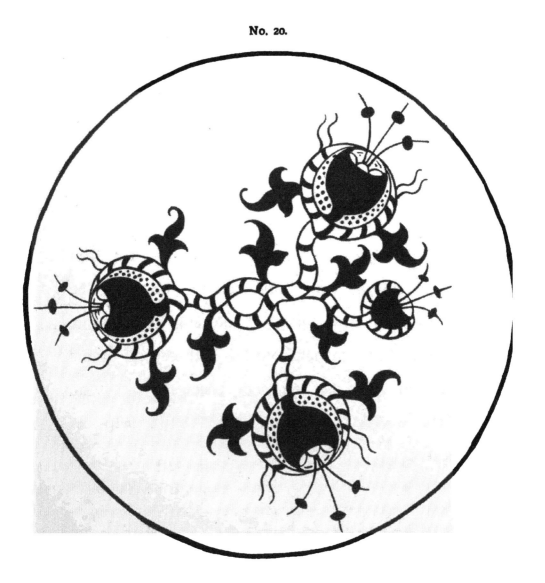

This "Moon and Star" design is suitable for Altar Frontals, &c. Can be either enlarged or reduced, according for what piece of work it is intended. The moons ought to be worked in gold, and the stars in silver; the petals to be worked in silk, any colour, or according to fancy; the stalk to be gold worked over string.

No. 21.

No. 22.

This "Ivy Leaf" design is suitable for Burse, Chalice Veil, end of Stoles, &c. The top of each leaf ought to have a bead or stone, the centre to be in gold, the leaves in colour to shade with whatever material it is worked on.

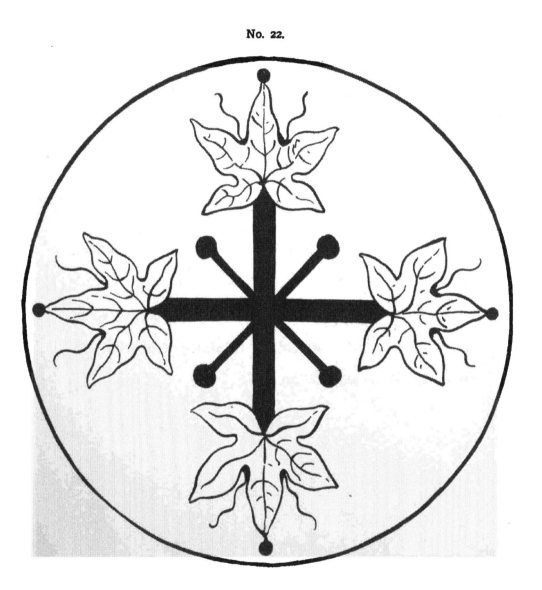

No. 23 represents a pomegranate springing as it were from a lily, and signifying Love and Purity. The design is one suitable for Altar Frontals, Burses, &c., &c. The pomegranate would look equally well treated in many different ways; and one arrangement that would lend itself to a quaint and pretty effect would be to place the pomegranate sideways, with a few of the seeds falling from it, to convey the idea of the abundant and abounding love emanating from purity, that "scattereth and yet increaseth."

It would be effective worked in corals and gold.

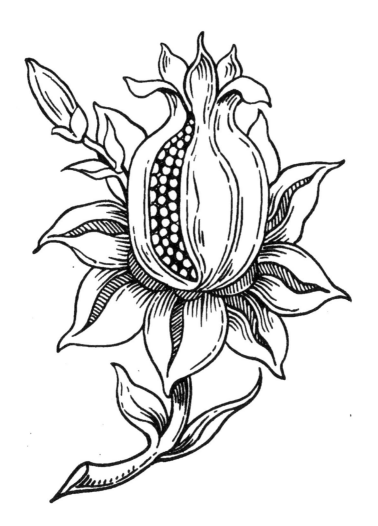

This design is suitable for Vestments, Altar Frontals, &c., &c., either enlarged or diminished, according to the size of work required.

The monogram ☧ stands for the name of Christ, and is formed of the two first Greek letters ☧ and Ρ of the word Christos. The lilies are the emblems of the Blessed Virgin, and signify purity.

This design would look well worked in white and gold on a green background, this colour being the one used by the Church on common Sundays and Ferias, or on ordinary week days. The monogram raised in gold, and the lilies white, would have a good effect.

The six following designs, for (25) Chasuble, (26) Chalice Veil, (27) Cope Hood, (28) Stole, (29) Burse, (30) Cope, are taken entirely from the instructions given in Exodus xxviii. for Aaron's vestments, made "for glory and for beauty." The description is minute and clear, and the one that has special reference to the bells and pomegranates, and suggested the design here given, occurs at verses 33, 34, and 35, and is as follows:—"And beneath upon the hem (or skirts) of it thou shalt make pomegranates of blue, and of purple, and of scarlet, round about the hem thereof; and bells of gold between them round about: a golden bell and a pomegranate, a golden bell and a pomegranate, upon the hem of the robe round about. And it shall be upon Aaron to minister: and his sound shall be heard when he goeth in unto the holy place before the Lord, and when he cometh out, that he die not."

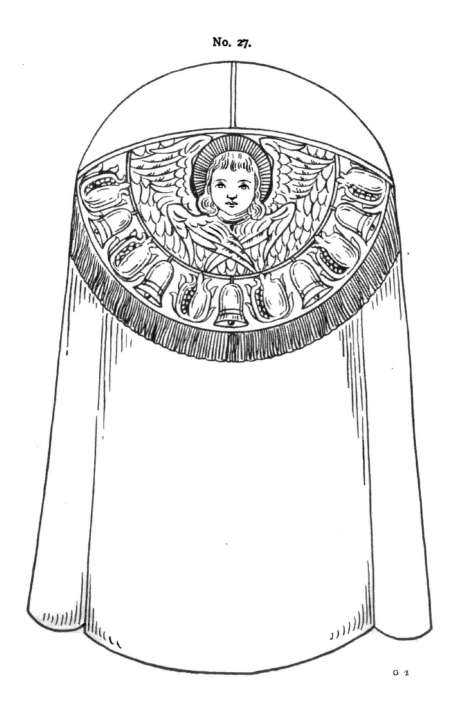

P

WORKS ON DESIGNING, ART, &c.,

PUBLISHED BY

CHAPMAN & HALL, Limited.

FRANK G. JACKSON.
THEORY AND PRACTICE OF DESIGN.
An Advanced Text-book on Decorative Art. By FRANK G. JACKSON. With 700 Illustrations. Crown 8vo. 9s.

FRANK G. JACKSON.
DECORATIVE DESIGN.
An Elementary Text-book of Principles and Practice. By F. G JACKSON. Fully Illustrated. Third Edition. Large crown 8vo. 7s. 6d.

JAMES WARD AND G. AITCHISON, A.R.A.
PRINCIPLES OF ORNAMENT.
By JAMES WARD. Edited by G. AITCHISON, A.R.A. Fully Illustrated. Crown 8vo. 7s. 6d.

JAMES WARD.
ELEMENTARY PRINCIPLES of ORNAMENT.
By JAMES WARD, Head Master of the Macclesfield School of Art. Fully Illustrated. Crown 8vo. 5s.

E. J. POYNTER, R.A.
TEN LECTURES ON ART.
By E. J. POYNTER, R.A. Third Edition. Large crown 8vo. 9s.

G. REDGRAVE.
OUTLINES OF HISTORIC ORNAMENT.
By G. REDGRAVE. Translated from the German. Edited by G. REDGRAVE. Crown 8vo. 4s.

R. N. WORNUM.
ANALYSIS OF ORNAMENT:
The Characteristics of Styles. An Introduction to the Study of the History of Ornamental Art. By R. N. WORNUM. Ninth Edition. Royal 8vo. 8s.

CHARLES RYAN.
EGYPTIAN ART:
An Elementary Handbook for the Use of Students. By CHARLES RYAN, late Head Master of the Ventnor School of Art. With 56 Illustrations. Crown 8vo. 2s. 6d.

RICHARD G. HATTON.
ELEMENTARY DESIGN:
Being a Theoretical and Practical Introduction in the Art of Decoration. By RICHARD G. HATTON, Durham College of Science, Newcastle-on-Tyne. With 110 Illustrations. Crown 8vo. 2s. 6d.

HISTORY OF ANCIENT ART BY GEORGES PERROT & CHARLES CHIPIEZ.

A HISTORY OF ANCIENT ART IN GREECE. With about 500 Illustrations. 2 vols.

A HISTORY OF ANCIENT ART IN PERSIA. With 254 Illustrations, and 12 Steel and Coloured Plates. Imperial 8vo. 21s.

A HISTORY OF ANCIENT ART IN PHRYGIA—LYDIA, and CARIA—LYCIA. With 280 Illustrations. Imperial 8vo. 15s.

A HISTORY OF ANCIENT ART IN SARDINIA, JUDÆA, SYRIA, and ASIA MINOR. With 395 Illustrations. 2 vols. Imperial 8vo. 36s.

A HISTORY OF ANCIENT ART IN PHŒNICIA AND ITS DEPENDENCIES. With 654 Illustrations. 2 vols. Imperial 8vo. 42s.

A HISTORY OF ART IN CHALDÆA AND ASSYRIA. With 452 Illustrations. 2 vols. Imperial 8vo. 42s.

A HISTORY OF ART IN ANCIENT EGYPT. With 600 Illustrations. 2 vols. Imperial 8vo. 42s.

SOUTH KENSINGTON MUSEUM ART HANDBOOKS

Published for the Committee of the Council on Education.

(A SELECTION.)

EARLY CHRISTIAN ART IN IRELAND.
By MARGARET STOKES. With 106 Woodcuts. Crown 8vo. 4s.

THE ART OF THE SARACENS IN EGYPT.
By STANLEY LANE POOLE, B.A., M.A.R.S. With 108 Woodcuts. Crown 8vo. 4s.

RUSSIAN ART AND ART OBJECTS IN RUSSIA:
A Handbook to the reproduction of Goldsmiths' Work and other Art Treasures from that country in the South Kensington Museum. By ALFRED MASKELL. With Illustrations. 4s. 6d.

INDUSTRIAL ARTS OF DENMARK.
From the Earliest Times to the Danish Conquest of England. By J. J. A. WORSAAE, Hon. F.S.A., &c., &c. With Map and Woodcuts. 3s. 6d.

INDUSTRIAL ARTS OF SCANDINAVIA
IN THE PAGAN TIME. By HANS HILDEBRAND, Royal Antiquary of Sweden. With numerous Woodcuts. 2s. 6d.

TAPESTRY.
By ALFRED DE CHAMPEAUX. With Woodcuts. 2s. 6d.

INDUSTRIAL ARTS OF INDIA.
By Sir GEORGE C. M. BIRDWOOD, C.S.I., &c. With Map and Woodcuts. Demy 8vo. 14s.

INDUSTRIAL ARTS IN SPAIN.
By JUAN F. RIAÑO. With numerous Woodcuts. 4s.

GOLD AND SILVER SMITHS' WORK.
By JOHN HUNGERFORD POLLEN, M.A. With numerous Woodcuts. 2s. 6d.

INDUSTRIAL ARTS:
Historical Sketches. With numerous Illustrations. 3s.

TEXTILE FABRICS.
By the Very Rev. DANIEL ROCK, D.D. With numerous Woodcuts. 2s. 6d.

MANUAL OF DESIGN.
By RICHARD REDGRAVE, R.A. By GILBERT R. REDGRAVE. With Woodcuts. 2s. 6d.

PERSIAN ART.
By Major R. MURDOCK SMITH, R.E. With Map and Woodcuts. Second Edition, enlarged. 2s.

CHAPMAN AND HALL, LIMITED, LONDON.